**Congressional
Research
Service**

Postsecondary Education Issues in the 113th Congress

David P. Smole, Coordinator
Specialist in Education Policy

November 7, 2013

Congressional Research Service

7-5700

www.crs.gov

R43302

CRS Report for Congress —————
Prepared for Members and Committees of Congress

Summary

The 113ᵗʰ Congress may face an array of policy issues affecting postsecondary education. Many of these postsecondary education issues may be considered as part of efforts to reauthorize the Higher Education Act of 1965, as amended (HEA). However, postsecondary education issues also may emerge as part of other legislative efforts such as comprehensive immigration reform (CIR), reform of the federal tax code, or the annual appropriations process.

This report identifies and briefly examines several postsecondary education policy issue areas that may be of general interest. For each of these broader issue areas, the report provides a brief background summary and an introduction to and discussion of various aspects of the issue. Varied policy options are also identified for further consideration. The following postsecondary education issue areas are examined in this report.

College costs and prices. What policy approaches are available that may help address concerns about ongoing increases in postsecondary education costs and the escalating prices colleges charge for tuition and fees?

The Federal Pell Grant program. What options might be considered to help ensure sustained funding for the Pell Grant program at current or other levels deemed to be adequate? Should changes be made to Pell Grant eligibility or award criteria to contain costs or otherwise adjust the targeting of aid?

Federal student loans. Are student loan terms and conditions and loan subsidy rates well aligned with program aims? Should policy options be considered that would affect the availability of loans, borrowing limits, interest rates, repayment relief, or the role of institutions of higher education in student borrowing?

Student loans and personal bankruptcy. Should all student loans continue to be excepted from discharge in bankruptcy, except in cases of undue hardship? What should constitute "undue hardship"?

Noncitizens and federal student aid. Should beneficiaries of comprehensive immigration reform legislation be granted eligibility to participate in HEA federal student aid programs?

Postsecondary education tax benefits. Are federal postsecondary education tax benefits appropriately targeted and effective in achieving their intended purposes? How do these benefits interact with traditional federal student aid?

Institutional quality. Should new institutional or programmatic eligibility requirements be considered to help ensure that recipients of federal student aid are obtaining a quality education from the institutions they attend? What would be appropriate standards for measuring or assessing institutional accountability for educational or student outcomes?

College completion. Are students completing college at desirable rates? Should new approaches be considered to further the aim of increasing college completion?

Campus safety. How might efforts to promote safety on college campuses be best supported while balancing the reporting and disclosure of campus safety information with the protection of student privacy?

Contents

Contacts

This report identifies and examines several of the major postsecondary education policy issues facing the 113th Congress. For each of the broader issue areas identified, the report provides brief background information and an introduction and discussion of various aspects of the issue. Varied policy options are also identified for further consideration. The aim of the report is to provide concise (2-4 page) summaries of selected postsecondary education policy issues and possible approaches to address them. The report does not attempt to thoroughly assess tradeoffs or possible advantages and disadvantages associated with the policy options that are discussed.

The federal government affects and influences postsecondary education policy most directly through the programs and policies authorized by the Higher Education Act of 1965, as amended (HEA; P.L. 89-329), and other federal postsecondary education programs, such as federal veterans' education benefits and federal tax benefits authorized under the Internal Revenue Code (IRC). Other federal laws also have an impact on postsecondary education policy. Examples include federal immigration laws and the federal bankruptcy code.

HEA programs and policies are particularly relevant at this time as the HEA may soon be considered for reauthorization. Authorization of appropriations for most HEA programs is provided through FY2014, with the General Education Provisions Act (GEPA) authorizing appropriations for an additional year—through FY2015. Many of the issues identified in this report may be considered as part of an HEA reauthorization effort.

Some of the other issues identified here have received recent legislative consideration or attention and may be considered as part of other legislative efforts before the 113th Congress. For example, issues pertaining to the education of noncitizens may be considered as part of legislative efforts related to comprehensive immigration reform (CIR). Issues pertaining to federal tax benefits supportive of postsecondary education may be considered as part of efforts to reform the IRC.

Postsecondary Education Issues in the 113th Congress

This report presents an examination of the following postsecondary education issue areas in the sections that follow.

- College costs and prices.
- The Federal Pell Grant program.
- Federal student loans.
- Student loans and personal bankruptcy.
- Noncitizens and eligibility for federal student aid.
- Postsecondary education tax benefits.
- Institutional quality.
- College completion.
- Campus safety.

College Costs and Prices[1]

The 113th Congress may consider policy options aimed at addressing college affordability. At issue is growing concern that college prices are becoming out of reach for many families.

In the United States, postsecondary education is financed through a mix of government appropriations, gift and endowment revenue, and payments for tuition and fees. In recent decades college prices have increased at rates that have consistently outpaced inflation.[2] With published prices for tuition, fees, room and board at public four-year institutions averaging roughly $17,000 for in-state students and $21,000 for out-of-state students, and $38,000 at private not-for-profit four-year institutions, concerns have arisen about college access and affordability and about the sustainability of further price increases.[3]

Myriad factors are thought to play a role in the escalation of college prices. Some commonly cited factors include the following:

- A decline in state higher education appropriations on a per student basis, which has led to greater reliance on tuition revenues at state colleges and universities.

- Fluctuating values of institutional endowments.

- Escalating costs of high-skilled labor which may have a particularly strong effect on higher education, a labor intensive industry that relies heavily on highly skilled labor.

- Escalating costs of technology and other goods that colleges update regularly.

- Durable demand for postsecondary education which may endow colleges, as credentialing institutions, with considerable pricing power (i.e., the ability to raise prices without destabilizing demand).

- A plurality of institutional missions at colleges and universities (which may divert attention and resources from instruction), and an orientation and incentives targeted toward raising and spending revenues to enhance the quality of students' experiences as opposed to a focus on utilizing revenues efficiently.

- Faculty governance, tenure policies, and ineffective central control of costs.

It has also been suggested that broad availability of and increases in federal financial aid for students may support or even fuel college price increases.

While a precise diagnosis of which among these factors play the primary roles in contributing to price increases remains elusive, there is little disagreement about the trends in prices, and about the increasing financial strain being placed on families and students pursuing postsecondary

---

[1] This section was prepared by Adam Stoll, astoll@crs.loc.gov, 7-4375.

[2] From 1991-1992 to 2011-2012 published cost of attendance at public four-year and private nonprofit four-year institutions of higher education outpaced inflation by an average of 2.2% and 1.9% each year, respectively. Source: CRS calculations using the Consumer Price Index-Urban (CPI-U) as a measure of inflation and data on trends in cost of attendance from the National Center for Education Statistics, *Digest of Education Statistics 2012*, Tables 349 & 350. These institutions tend to be the focus of much of the dialogue about college affordability.

[3] U.S. Department of Education, Institute of Education Sciences, National Center for Education Statistics, *Digest of Education Statistics 2012*, Tables 349 & 350.

---

education. At the same time, there is no clear roadmap toward a solution. However, the levers available to federal policymakers—should they seek to address affordability—provide many options. Some of the options that receive frequent mention and relevant considerations are discussed below.

Address Imperfections in Consumer Information

Student aid programs authorized under the Higher Education Act of 1965, as amended (HEA; P.L. 89-329) generally provide portable aid which is premised on empowering students to shop on the basis of quality and price among qualified institutions in the higher education marketplace. In a properly functioning market, it is assumed that consumers have good information about the goods and services they are purchasing. However, imperfect information is commonly identified as a problem affecting students seeking to choose among colleges and college programs.

An example of this is a perceived lack of transparency regarding college prices. While colleges publish list prices, they also engage in fairly extensive tuition discounting on the basis of factors such as need and merit. These discounts, in effect, reduce prices.[4] Additionally, other subsidies such as governmental grants, also often awarded on the basis of need, further defray the price students are actually asked to pay. Since "net prices" (prices net of governmental grant aid and institutional discounts) are not available to students when they are applying to schools, students must often determine the schools they are going to apply to without having a clear sense of the price they will actually be asked to pay, and without the ability to compare prices between different institutions. Moreover, multi-year prices for educational programs are generally not available when students are identifying college choices and when selecting a college to attend.

This lack of transparency results in part because the net price for each individual is determined annually and is influenced by factors such as financial need and merit which can fluctuate across candidates and across years in school. Net price is also affected by factors such as the non-tuition revenue available to schools which fluctuates across years.

The federal government has taken some steps through provisions enacted in the Higher Education Opportunity Act of 2008 (HEOA; P.L. 110-315) to address transparency issues. These provisions require colleges to make available more information on net prices charged in recent years to different categories of students, and require schools to post on-line net price calculators.[5] Still, the required net price information delineates existing net prices across a fairly limited set of students (e.g., only for aided students), and net price calculators are criticized sometimes for lacking sophistication and/or being cumbersome to use. It has been suggested that requiring more comprehensive data, different data, or different displays of data on institutional net prices and discounts across categories of students might be helpful, and that net price calculators or "estimators" with greater functionality or that are easier to use might also be desirable.[6] Further, it

---

[4] For more information on tuition discount rates at public and private nonprofit institutions of higher education, see *Revenues: Where Does the Money Come From?*, Delta Cost Project, American Institutes of Research, Rita Kirshtein and Steven Hurlburt, 2012, Figure 3. In 2010, at four-year institutions, tuition discount rates ranged from 12% at public master's institutions to 36% at private bachelor's institutions.

[5] Other HEOA innovations include the creation of the Department of Education's College Affordability and Transparency Center, which annually makes available information on trends in college net and list prices along with the College Scorecard, http://collegecost.ed.gov/scorecard/, which posts information about college's affordability and value.

[6] See "Wellesley College Offers Easy Estimator of What Families Might Pay", *The Chronicle of Higher Education*, (continued...)

---

is sometimes suggested that in addition to year one net price estimates, admitted students might be provided net price estimates or ranges for the full program that are grounded in the known characteristics of the students (and family) that are likely to affect calculated need and thus impact net price across multiple years in school (such as variation brought on by fluctuation in the number of family members expected to be enrolled in college).

Another component of consumer information that has garnered attention is information on student outcomes. In a variety of venues there have been calls for improvements in the availability and quality of information on employment and earnings outcomes for college graduates and for graduates of specific academic programs. This information is not consistently available, making it hard for students to gauge potential return on educational investments. Data collection and reporting on student outcomes for institutions or specific academic programs could be supported, facilitated and/or required by the federal government. This could be a large undertaking and depending on the approach employed also may raise privacy concerns.

Better information on price and student outcomes may enable students to make better informed decisions about how much to invest in educational programs and about which programs to pursue, which may in turn have an effect on prices.

Provide Incentives for Colleges to Contain Price Increases

Proposals have been considered in recent years that would tie participation in certain federal student aid programs to an institution's rate of increase in prices. Generally these types of proposals constrain access to new or existing student aid programs for colleges whose prices rise at levels beyond some type of college affordability index which is constructed based on a measure of inflation such as the consumer price index for all urban consumers (CPI-U). These types of proposals can also be structured in ways that provide access to more aid at schools whose price increases fare well in relation to a college affordability index. In general, these proposals have targeted aid awarded directly to colleges, such as the HEA campus-based programs or newly proposed student aid funds that would be awarded directly to colleges. Provided that the incentives to control prices are sufficiently robust, they might induce colleges to focus on constraining those expenditures and practices that contribute to price increases over which they have control.

Facilitate or Accommodate the Growth of Nontraditional Educational Programs and Service Providers

Traditionally, higher education has been a labor-intensive endeavor, placing a high priority on preserving limited-scale interactions between instructors and students. It has been commonly argued that given the nature of the service being provided, opportunities to substitute technology for labor are limited. In recent years, however, the rapid expansion of online education programs and courses may be beginning to challenge this notion. One development has been the growth of online college courses and programs, with an estimated 6.7 million students enrolled in at least

---

(...continued)

Head Count, September 18, 2013, for an example of an estimator that has received some attention recently.

one online course at degree-granting institutions. Online courses and programs are available at a large share of the nation's colleges and universities.[7]

If taught like traditional courses, these on-line offerings seemingly do not do much to reduce costs. However, some instructional models have been developed that draw on specialists in content and instructional design and assessment to develop courses and use lower cost staff to coach students and monitor their progress. For introductory classes and certain types of other courses—and even certain types of academic programs—this approach may achieve economies of scale without compromising quality.

Another recent development has been the emergence of so-called massive open online courses (MOOCs) being offered by numerous colleges and universities, including many of the nation's most selective and well-known colleges. MOOCs, which are generally free online versions of college courses, by some estimates boast 4 million registrants, although a relatively small percentage of registrants reportedly complete their courses.[8] MOOCs are being looked at as options for addressing overflow demand for introductory courses in some public systems. Some thought has also been given to offering college credit or certificates signifying successful completion of MOOC coursework contingent upon passing assessments. The exact role of online courses and programs and their potential for lowering costs is very much evolving and difficult to estimate at this stage.

A federal role in helping to facilitate or accommodate the growth of these nontraditional programs and services could take many shapes, but it is likely to at a minimum involve examining HEA Title IV institutional eligibility rules which define educational programs and courses in ways that are not always in synch with the way these courses and programs are delivered and participated in. If higher education innovators are finding creative ways to cut costs, regulation will likely remain important to help ensure program quality, but may have to be adaptable so as not to serve as a barrier to institutions developing lower cost approaches for providing instruction to students.

Scale Back or Refocus the Targeting of Federal Student Aid and Education Benefits

Federal student aid is the primary source of aid provided directly to students and their families, comprising roughly 75% of such aid.[9] In policy and academic circles it is sometimes suggested that federal student aid may fuel or at least enable increases in college prices (e.g., that it would be difficult to continue to increase prices at rates exceeding inflation without widespread access to student loans and other federal education benefits). Further it is sometimes argued that limiting the availability of federal financial assistance might place downward pressure on college prices if the restrictions have the effect of limiting students' and families' ability to draw upon federal benefits in lieu of paying college expenses with resources from savings or current income.

If policymakers sought to address concerns that the availability of some forms of assistance may facilitate price increases, these concerns might be addressed through a reexamination of the

---

[7] *Changing Course: Ten Years of Tracking Online Education in the United States*, January 2013, I. Elaine Allen and Jeff Seaman, Babson Survey Research Group.

[8] Stephanie Wang, "Free Online Classes Bring Higher Education to the Masses*", Indianapolis Star*, March 7, 2013.

[9] *Trends in Student Aid 2012*, College Board, p.10. This figure is from academic year 2010-2011 and includes federal student loans, grants, work study, veterans and military education benefits, and education tax benefits.

policies through which the various forms of assistance are made available. For example, the targeting of federal financial aid could be refocused or scaled back in numerous ways. Options might involve the elimination of certain types of aid, adjustments to benefit levels (e.g., grant amounts) or aid availability (e.g., loan limits), and adjustments to aid recipient eligibility criteria. Other options for refocusing or scaling back aid might include adjustments to the rules pertaining to the allowable educational expenses aid awards can cover. Among the ways this might be approached is through decoupling student aid awards from institutional cost of attendance (COA), which is set by colleges under existing HEA provisions, and serves as the maximum amount that federal student aid can be used to cover.

While there are many possible approaches toward reducing or refocusing aid, few proposals have been forwarded in recent years to do so on a large scale with the stated aim of helping to contain prices. This may be due to anticipated tradeoffs which include the potential for adversely affecting college access and attainment which have long been of central importance to federal policy in this area.

Federal Pell Grant Program: Short-Term Funding Needs in FY2015 and Long-Term Program Reform[10]

The 113th Congress may consider ways to address the need for additional discretionary funding for the Pell Grant program in the current fiscal year (FY) to ensure the current maximum benefits are maintained beginning in FY2015. Additionally, to help improve the program's long-term discretionary funding outlook under current baseline projections and spending limitations enacted as part of the Budget Control Act of 2011 (P.L. 112-25; BCA), Congress may consider myriad reforms to the program. These reforms may be considered incrementally over the near-term, or as part of a larger comprehensive effort aimed at changing federal student aid programs under the reauthorization of the HEA.

Background

The Federal Pell Grant program,[11] authorized by Title IV of the HEA, is the single largest source of federal grant aid supporting postsecondary education students. The program provided approximately $31.7 billion to approximately 9.1 million undergraduate students in FY2012.[12] The program is estimated to have provided over $33.5 billion to approximately 9.7 million undergraduate students in FY2011.[13] Pell Grants are need-based aid that is intended to be the foundation for all federal student aid awarded to undergraduates. There is no absolute income threshold that determines who is eligible or ineligible for Pell Grants. Nevertheless, Pell Grant recipients are primarily low-income. In FY2011, an estimated 74% of all Pell Grant recipients had a total family income at or below $30,000.

---

[10] This section was prepared by Shannon M. Mahan, smahan@crs.loc.gov, 7-7759.

[11] For additional information on the Federal Pell Grant Program, see CRS Report R42446, *Federal Pell Grant Program of the Higher Education Act: How the Program Works, Recent Legislative Changes, and Current Issues*, by Shannon M. Mahan.

[12] U.S. Department of Education, Federal Student Aid Data Center. Available online at http://studentaid.ed.gov/about/data-center/student/title-iv.

[13] U.S. Department of Education, unpublished data.

For award year (AY) 2013-2014, which began July 1, 2013,[14] the total maximum Pell Grant award is $5,645.[15] Of this amount, the base discretionary award ($4,860 in FY2013), is funded with and determined by the annual appropriations process. An additional amount that is added to the base discretionary award, known as the mandatory add-on award ($785 in FY2013), is determined each year by a formula included in the HEA and is funded with indefinite mandatory appropriations. While mandatory appropriations have played a larger role in funding the program in recent years, the program is funded primarily through annual discretionary appropriations. All funding for the Pell Grant program is exempt from across-the-board cuts, known as budget sequestration, under the BCA in current and future years.[16]

As of May 2013, the Congressional Budget Office (CBO) estimated the program would experience a substantial funding surplus in FY2014 due to less demand in the program and the availability of mandatory funds to augment discretionary appropriations, which were provided in previous laws. The availability of surplus funds in FY2014 increases the likelihood that the discretionary base maximum award will be able to be maintained at $4,860 in AY2014-2015.[17] In FY2015, however, CBO baseline estimates show the potential for a discretionary funding gap of approximately $800 million, which is the difference between the estimated cost of the program in AY2015-2016 at current maximum benefit levels and the estimated available funding for the program, which assumes the recent FY2013 funding level and the projected funding surplus from FY2014.[18]

Beyond FY2015, CBO baseline estimates suggest that if future discretionary funding levels are maintained at recent FY2013 funding levels without adjusting for inflation and the current discretionary base maximum award is maintained in each year, the program would experience an annual average funding gap of $5.8 billion from FY2016 to FY2023. The potential for long-term funding challenges under the spending limitations imposed on overall discretionary spending under the BCA, along with recently enacted policy changes aimed primarily at Pell Grant program cost reduction, have led some analysts to call for broader reforms that may address some of the long-standing critiques and emerging issues in the program and higher education policy in general.

Pell Grant Policy Options

The 113th Congress may explore reform options for the Pell Grant program as part of a cost-savings package to ensure adequate funding is provided in FY2015 to continue current maximum benefits, or it may consider broader policy reforms that have implications for the program over the long-term, perhaps as part of reauthorization of the HEA. Some of the options that may garner

---

[14] Award year 2013-14 will end on June 30, 2014.

[15] U.S. Department of Education, Federal Student Aid, Dear Colleague Letter GEN-13-06, "2013-2014 Federal Pell Grant Payment and Disbursement Schedules", January 30, 2013.

[16] For more information on how sequestration will affect other federal student aid programs, see U.S. Department of Education, Office of Postsecondary Education, Electronic Announcement, "Update: Impact of Sequestration on the Title IV Student Financial Assistance Programs", Mar. 15, 2013.

[17] The add-on mandatory award is projected to be $925 in AY2014-2015; the total maximum award in AY2014-2015 is projected to be $5,785

[18] Congressional Budget Office, "Federal Pell Grant Program, Discretionary Baseline, Cumulative Surplus/Shortfall, Funding Gap", May 13, 2013.

consideration and factors that might be taken into account when considering potential reform options include the following:

Eligibility for and Targeting of Pell Grant Aid

- Should students who enroll on a less-than-half time basis continue to be eligible for reduced Pell Grant aid?

- Should full-time enrollment for the purposes of receiving Pell Grant aid continue to be defined as 12 credit hours (or the equivalent) per semester, as compared to a more intensive enrollment criterion, such as 15 credit hours (or the equivalent)? If the standard for full-time enrollment was made more rigorous, how would institutions respond to this change, and how might this change affect persistence for Pell Grant recipients?

- Should the current process for applying for Pell Grant aid and determining eligibility be streamlined or simplified? Could eligibility for and the distribution of aid be determined based on an existing federal proxy for low-income families, such as the Department of Health and Human Services (HHS) poverty guidelines?

- Could changes to the need analysis methodology be implemented that would more accurately reflect the current family financial situations of Pell Grant applicants? Could Pell Grant aid be more targeted to low-income students through need analysis changes?

Funding for the Pell Grant Program

- How does the current funding structure of the Pell Grant program (i.e., a base maximum award funded with discretionary appropriations and a mandatory add-on award funded with indefinite mandatory appropriations) contribute to the long-term funding challenges for the program? Could the current funding structure be changed to ensure students continue to receive annual increases in the Pell Grant maximum award, while both eliminating future add-on mandatory awards and stabilizing discretionary funding? Under current estimates, the program will require additional discretionary appropriations to maintain the current base discretionary maximum award in future years, while the HEA provides for future annual increases in the add-on award through indefinite mandatory appropriations. Overall discretionary appropriations may continue to be constrained under the BCA, which may affect the amount and purchasing power of the Pell Grant in the short-term, despite mandatory increases in the add-on award amounts over the long-term budget window. Could indefinite mandatory appropriations currently available in future years for the add-on award be redirected to supplement annual discretionary appropriations and increase the base maximum award in the short term? Conversely, could the program be converted to a full entitlement for budgetary purposes?

- Should Congress continue to look for cost savings in the federal student loan programs as a way to provide additional funding for the Pell Grant program? If so, what types of changes should be made to the federal loan programs and how might potential reductions in federal loan subsidies affect students who also receive Pell Grant aid?

Program Administration and Accountability

- Should institutions of higher education (IHEs) continue to receive an annual administrative cost allowance fee of $5 per Pell Grant recipient? If not, should IHEs be compensated in other ways to account for the administrative burdens imposed by the program rules, regulations, and reporting requirements?

- Should IHEs and/or students be required to meet certain outcome metrics (e.g., graduation rates, job placement rates, or cost reduction targets) in order to receive (or continue to receive) Pell Grant aid? If so, how might these outcome metrics be calculated and should these measures apply similarly to different types of IHEs? How might IHEs respond to these requirements? How would certain outcome measures affect postsecondary access for Pell Grant recipients?

Federal Student Loans[19]

Federal student loans constitute the largest source of federal student aid made available through programs authorized under the HEA. Millions of students and their families rely on federal student loans to help finance their postsecondary education expenses. The number of federal student loan borrowers continues to grow and since loans are repaid over a period that typically spans a decade or more, federal student loan policy affects a growing share of the general population. While numerous changes have been made to the federal student loan programs in recent years, the 113th Congress may explore whether current federal student loan policy is optimal or whether additional changes should be considered, such as those that would affect loan terms and conditions, program administration, or program costs.

Background

Federal student loans are currently made through two programs administered by the U.S. Department of Education (ED)—the William D. Ford Federal Direct Loan (Direct Loan) program[20] and the Federal Perkins Loan program[21]. ED also continues to administer the Federal Family Education Loan (FFEL) program, through which a set of federally guaranteed student loans with similar terms and conditions to those offered through the Direct Loan program were made until June 30, 2010. The following types of loans are currently available to borrowers through the Direct Loan and Federal Perkins Loan programs:

- Direct Subsidized Loans, which are need-based loans available only to undergraduate students.

- Direct Unsubsidized Loans, which are non-need-based loans available to undergraduate students, and to graduate and professional students.

---

[19] This section was prepared by David P. Smole, dsmole@crs.loc.gov, 7-0624.

[20] For additional information on loans made through the Direct Loan program, see CRS Report R40122, *Federal Student Loans Made Under the Federal Family Education Loan Program and the William D. Ford Federal Direct Loan Program: Terms and Conditions for Borrowers*, by David P. Smole.

[21] For additional information on loans made through the Federal Perkins Loan program, see CRS Report RL31618, *Campus-Based Student Financial Aid Programs Under the Higher Education Act*, by David P. Smole and Alexandra Hegji.

- Direct PLUS Loans, which are non-need-based loans available to graduate and professional students, and to parents of undergraduate students who are dependent upon their parents for financial support.

- Federal Perkins Loans, which are need-based loans available to undergraduate students, and to graduate and professional students.

- Direct Consolidation Loans, which are available to existing borrowers of federal student loans, and which may be used to combine one or more loans into a single loan and to extend the repayment term.

In recent years, numerous changes have been made that affect the terms, conditions, and availability of federal student loans.[22] Graduate and professional students were extended eligibility to borrow PLUS Loans beginning with award year (AY) 2007-2008; and beginning with AY2012-2013, they lost eligibility to borrow Direct Subsidized Loans. Annual borrowing limits were increased for undergraduate students in AY2007-2008; and in AY2008-2009 both annual and aggregate borrowing limits were increased for undergraduate students. The income-based repayment (IBR) plan became available to borrowers of FFEL and Direct Loans in 2008; and the Pay-As-You-Earn (PAYE) repayment plan became available to borrowers of Direct Loans in 2012. Also, in 2007, borrowers of Direct Loans became eligible to begin qualifying for a new Public Service Loan Forgiveness program. The statutorily-specified interest rates applicable to Subsidized Loans made to undergraduate students were incrementally lowered over a period of several years from a fixed rate of 6.8% that applies to loans made during AY2008-2009 to a fixed rate of 3.4% that applies to loans made during AY2011-2012 and AY2012-2013. Beginning with AY2013-2014, all types of Direct Loans are now being made with market-indexed, fixed interest rates.

Federal student loan borrowing has increased substantially in recent years. In FY2007, a combined total of $65 billion in federal student loans were made through the Direct Loan, Federal Perkins Loan, and FFEL programs to students and their parents to help them finance their postsecondary education expenses. By FY2013, annual borrowing through the Direct Loan and Federal Perkins Loan programs had increased to an estimated combined total of $107 billion.[23]

The recent increase in federal student loan borrowing reflects an increase in the number and proportion of students who borrow annually as well as the amounts they borrow. In AY2007-2008, 34.7% of undergraduate students borrowed federal student loans; and the average amount borrowed that year was $5,100.[24] In AY2011-2012, the percentage of undergraduate students who borrowed federal student loans had increased to 40.2%; and the average amount borrowed had increased to $6,500.[25]

---

[22] A comprehensive description of the terms and conditions of FFEL and Direct Loans is presented in CRS Report R40122, *Federal Student Loans Made Under the Federal Family Education Loan Program and the William D. Ford Federal Direct Loan Program: Terms and Conditions for Borrowers*, by David P. Smole.

[23] U.S. Department of Education, *FY2009 and FY2014 Justifications of Appropriation Estimates to the Congress*. These figures exclude Consolidation Loans.

[24] U.S. Department of Education, National Center for Education Statistics, "Student Financing of Undergraduate Education: 2007-08," (NCES 2010-162), Table 3.2-A and Table 3.2-B.

[25] U.S. Department of Education, National Center for Education Statistics, "2011-12 National Postsecondary Student Aid Study (NPSAS:12): Student Financial Aid Estimates for 2011-12," (NCES 2013-165), Table 3 and Table 4.

As the amount of federal student loans borrowed each year continues to grow, so does the combined total outstanding balance of federal student loans. At the end of FY2007, the combined outstanding balance of FFEL, DL and Perkins Loans totaled $516 billion. By the end of the 3^(rd) quarter of FY2013, the combined total outstanding balance of federal student loans made through these programs had surpassed $1 trillion.[26] Aggregate student loan debt is now the nation's second largest source of consumer debt, following mortgage debt. More than 38 million individuals currently have outstanding federal student loan debt. Many of these borrowers are experiencing difficulty repaying their student loans. In recent years, student loan delinquencies and defaults have increased.

The Direct Loan program is classified as a federal credit program for budgeting purposes. Most of the costs to the government associated with the program are accounted for on an accrual basis according to criteria specified in the Federal Credit Reform Act of 1990 (FCRA; P.L. 101-508), although the costs of administering the program are accounted for separately on a cash basis. Under FCRA, the net present value of future credit flows associated with federal student loans are discounted to the fiscal year in which the loans are made using interest rates on Treasury securities with comparable maturities; and these discounted credit flows are expressed as loan subsidy rates. The loan subsidy rates reflect the difference between the cost to the government of making student loans and the amounts the government receives as the loans are repaid. According to CBO's latest projections, for the foreseeable future loans made through the Direct Loan program will have negative subsidy rates.[27] In other words, as accounted for according to rules specified under the FCRA, the government expects to earn more through the Direct Loan program than the amount it costs to make the loans.

Issues

The 113^(th) Congress may explore options for making changes to federal student loan policies. A number of broader issues related to the federal student loan programs are identified and discussed below.

Simplify or Streamline Federal Student Loan Offerings

At present, two HEA federal student loan programs make available five types of loans and serve three broad classes of borrowers. The 113^(th) Congress may consider whether the currently available mix of loan programs and loan types is optimal or whether these loan programs and loan types, and their availability to different classes of borrowers, should be reconfigured. Need-based, Direct Subsidized Loans are available only to undergraduate students, while need-based Perkins Loans are available to undergraduate, graduate, and professional students. (For both these need-based loan types, no interest accrues on the loans while the borrower is in school nor while the loans are in deferment.) Non-need-based Direct Unsubsidized Loans are available to undergraduate, graduate, and professional students; and non-need-based Direct PLUS Loans are available to graduate and professional students and to the parents of undergraduate dependent students. Among the questions that arise about the varied loan types available are the following.

---

[26] U.S. Department of Education, Federal Student Aid Data Center, National Student Loan Data System (NSLDS), "Federal Student Aid Portfolio Summary".

[27] Congressional Budget Office, "CBO May 2013 Baseline Projections for the Student Loan Program," May 14, 2013; and Congressional Budget Office, "Subsidy Rates for Student Loans Under the May 2013 Baseline And As Adjusted for Enactment of P.L. 113-28, the Bipartisan Student Loan Certainty Act of 2013," August 12, 2013.

Should the availability of each of these loan types be continued in their current form? Should Direct Subsidized Loans—which have the highest loan subsidy costs and are available only to undergraduate students—continue to be made? Should authorization for the Perkins Loan program, a revolving loan fund, be extended so the program can continue to operate alongside the Direct Loan program?[28]

Adjust Borrowing Limits

The amounts that individuals may borrow in federal student loans are determined according to a complicated set of criteria and factors that differ by loan program, loan type, and class of borrower, and are dependent upon the cost of attendance (COA) of the student's school, the amount of other financial assistance the student receives, and—for need-based loans—the student's expected family contribution (EFC). Loans made through the Direct Loan program are entitlements to qualified borrowers while financial aid officers have some discretion in how they award Perkins Loans. At present, annual borrowing limits range from the comparatively low annual loan limits for Direct Subsidized Loans to undergraduate students (e.g., $3,500 for first year students) to expansive limits for PLUS Loans made to graduate and professional students and parent borrowers (e.g., COA, minus other financial assistance received). Cumulative borrowing limits for Direct Subsidized and Unsubsidized Loans, combined, range from $31,000 for undergraduate dependent students, to $138,500 for graduate and professional students. There are no specified cumulative borrowing limits for PLUS Loans. Separate borrowing limits apply for Perkins Loans. Existing borrowing limits attempt to balance the aims of preventing students from over-borrowing early in their academic careers and making federal student loans widely available to more senior students and parents who might otherwise turn to private education loans or other financing methods that typically have less favorable terms and conditions.

Issues pertaining to borrowing limits stem from varied concerns. Some are focused on the amounts of debt being incurred by borrowers, while others are focused on ensuring students and their families can continue to meet rising college prices. Still others are focused on the possibility that the availability of open-ended or broad borrowing opportunities may enable college price increases. Among the questions that arise are the following. Should federal policies for establishing the amounts that individuals may borrow in federal student loans be revised? For example, should financial aid administrators be granted expanded authority to limit borrowing by certain individuals to amounts lower than currently specified statutory maximum borrowing limits? Should individuals continue to be permitted to borrow non-need-based federal student loans to finance expenses that, according to federal need analysis rules, would otherwise be met by their expected family contribution? Should specific borrowing limits be established for PLUS Loans?

Adjust Interest Rates and Refinancing Opportunities

The Bipartisan Student Loan Certainty Act of 2013 (P.L. 113-28) made major changes to student loan interest rates. Beginning with AY2013-2014, rates on Direct Loans are being set according to a market-indexed, fixed interest rate formula. Rates on these loans are indexed to the yield on 10-year U.S. Treasury Notes, plus an interest rate premium, or add-on, which differs by loan type.

---

[28] The Perkins Loan program is authorized through FY2014 under HEA, §461(b); and one-year extension of the program (through FY2015) is authorized under the General Education Provisions Act (GEPA), §422(a).

Interest rate caps limit maximum rates. The rate in effect at the time a loan is made stays in effect for the duration of the loan. The changes enacted by P.L. 113-28, however, do not affect loans made prior to AY2013-2014.

The market-indexed, fixed rate structure enacted under P.L. 113-28 aligns borrower rates with market conditions at the time a loan is made, and these rates remain in effect for the life of the loan. This is somewhat similar to the way rates are set on some other loan types, such as fixed rate mortgages. The fixed rate structure insulates borrowers against fluctuations in market rates that might occur after their loans are made. This aspect of the rate structure is favorable to those who borrow when rates are low, but may be unfavorable to those who borrow when rates are high. For instance, unlike some other types of fixed rate loans, such as mortgages, the Direct Loan program does not provide an option for borrowers to refinance their loans should market rates subsequently drop. The recently enacted market-indexed, fixed rate structure applies only to new loans made during AY2013-2014 and future years; it does not affect loans made in recent years with interest rates above the rates at which new loans are currently being made.

Borrower interest rates have been adjusted multiple times in recent years as policymakers have sought to find a desirable balance between providing low-cost financing opportunities to students and their families and limiting the federal government's budgetary costs. Interest rate deliberations often involve consideration of the magnitude of the loan subsidy to be provided by the federal government; and when changes are made to loan terms, the extent that the loan subsidy rate changes from the baseline. Questions that commonly arise during interest rate deliberations include the following. To what extent should the federal government issue loans that have negative subsidy rates? Should borrowers of fixed interest rate federal student loans made during periods when rates were comparatively high be afforded the opportunity to refinance their loans during periods when market rates are low? If providing borrowers with an opportunity to refinance their loans would result in higher loan subsidy rates, how should the increased costs to the government be offset?

Strengthening Institutional Accountability for Student Loans

Under current law, student loan cohort default rates are one measure designed to hold institutions accountable for the repayment of federal student loans borrowed by students to finance their costs of attendance. Cohort default rates measure the percentage of borrowers who default within a certain period after beginning the repayment of their loans. A measurement period of three fiscal years is used for official cohort default rates for borrowers of certain Direct Loans and FFEL program loans;[29] a period of two fiscal years is used for Perkins Loan cohort default rates. PLUS Loans are not considered in the calculation of official cohort default rates. Schools with high cohort default rates may lose eligibility to continue to participate in the Direct Loan and Federal Pell Grant programs.

Over the course of the past several years, the Department of Education has sought to establish additional institutional student loan-based accountability measures through the regulatory process, which it refers to as 'gainful employment' measures. Among other things, the gainful employment measures would examine the student loan debt-to-earnings ratios of students who

---

[29] A change from a two fiscal year to a three fiscal year cohort default rate measurement period was enacted under the Higher Education Opportunity Act of 2008 (HEOA; P.L. 110-315). The first three-year official cohort default rates were published in 2012 for borrowers who entered repayment in FY2009.

complete certain programs. ED has initiated a second round of negotiated rulemaking to establish gainful employment measures after the regulations it initially adopted were successfully challenged in federal court.

Issues related to institutional accountability often arise in the context of seeking to ensure that both federal subsidies for postsecondary education programs and students' individual investments in those programs are sound. Among the issues that arise are the following. To what extent, if any, should institutions be held accountable for the repayment of the federal student loans borrowed to finance the costs of the programs they offer? Should PLUS Loans, which have open-ended borrowing limits, be included in the calculation of cohort default rates? If institutions are to be held accountable for the repayment of student loans, should they also be granted more discretion in limiting the amounts that individuals may borrow? Can new student loan accountability measures be developed and implemented in a manner that does not unduly affect institutions that serve large proportions of disadvantaged students?

Streamlining, Scaling Back, or Expanding Repayment Relief Programs

The terms and conditions of federal student loans provide borrowers with flexible repayment options and numerous forms of repayment relief. A selection of loan repayment plans allow borrowers to vary the size of their loan payments and the length of their repayment term; and with some plans, to limit the amounts they are required to pay based on their income. In particular, a more generous version of the income-based repayment (IBR) plan becomes available to new borrowers as of October 1, 2014; and the Pay-As-You-Earn (PAYE) repayment plan—which has similar terms—recently became available to some borrowers. Direct Consolidation Loans afford borrowers the opportunity to consolidate one or more loans into a single Direct Consolidation Loan and to lower their monthly loan payments by extending the repayment term. Deferments and forbearance allow borrowers to temporarily suspend the repayment of their loans. A large array of loan forgiveness and loan repayment programs provide borrowers means to have all or part of their student loans forgiven or repaid in exchange for work or service in specific fields or professions or based on their financial circumstances. Federal student loans are discharged in the case of borrower total and permanently disability or death. While numerous forms of repayment relief are available to borrowers, many still become delinquent or default on their loans.

Some of the issues pertaining to forms of repayment relief relate to the desire to provide help to borrowers—who are increasingly taking on higher levels of debt—when they experience some type of economic hardship. Others pertain to concerns that there may be too many disparate repayment relief benefits and that streamlining them may result in a more coherent approach toward providing assistance. Additionally, some of the issues that arise pertain to the extent that subsidies should be provided to borrowers once they have completed school. Some of the issues that arise concerning repayment relief include the following.

Should the availability of repayment plans such as IBR and PAYE be extended to a broader class of borrowers? Should eligible borrowers be automatically placed in these repayment plans rather than being required to opt in? Are these repayment plans too generous; and if so, should their availability or their benefits be curtailed? Are the numerous loan forgiveness and loan repayment programs accomplishing their aims? As currently designed, do these programs focus debt relief on targeted classes of borrowers in support of policy objectives? Do some of these programs create an incentive for individuals to borrow more than they otherwise would? Should these programs be streamlined into fewer or more narrowly targeted programs?

Student Loans and Personal Bankruptcy[30]

Generally, student loans cannot be discharged in bankruptcy. This has been true for all except private student loans since 1998. Beginning with bankruptcy petitions filed after October 16, 2005, private student loans were similarly barred from discharge in bankruptcy. However, in limited circumstances, any student loan may be discharged in bankruptcy. Such discharge requires a showing that failure to discharge the loan "would impose an undue hardship on the debtor and the debtor's dependents."[31]

Currently two issues appear to predominate in the area of student loans and bankruptcy. The first is whether all student loans, including private loans, should generally be excepted from discharge in bankruptcy. The second involves the "undue hardship" standard that allows discharge of student loans.

Should All Student Loans Be Excepted from Discharge in Bankruptcy?

The 113th Congress may explore the treatment of student loans in bankruptcy proceedings. The Bankruptcy Abuse Prevention and Consumer Protection Act of 2005 (BAPCPA) changed the way that private student loans were treated in bankruptcy. Prior to October 17, 2005 (the effective date for most provisions in BAPCPA), private student loans could be discharged in bankruptcy in the same way as most other unsecured debt. The legislative history for BAPCPA contains no obvious reason behind the change in the treatment of private student loans. In hearings held by both Senate[32] and House[33] committees, some witnesses asserted that, due to higher interest rates and less flexible repayment provisions, private student loans may cause greater fiscal distress to the borrower. Others maintained that student loans are inherently different than other unsecured debt and that making them dischargeable in bankruptcy would result in both fewer lenders and higher interest rates. Legislation introduced in the 111th and 112th Congresses is discussed in "Revisiting the Treatment of Private Student Loans and Other Educational Benefits in Bankruptcy."[34]

What Constitutes "Undue Hardship"?

The 113th Congress may also consider what constitutes "undue hardship" and whether it should be explicitly defined. Although many terms used within the U.S. Bankruptcy Code[35] are defined in §101, "undue hardship" is not among the terms defined. Neither is it defined within §523(a)(8) where it is set as the standard for allowing discharge of student loans that are, otherwise, barred from discharge. The courts have attempted to fill this void by formulating their own definition of

---

[30] This section was prepared by Carol A. Pettit, cpettit@crs.loc.gov, 7-9496.

[31] 11 U.S.C. §523(a)(8).

[32] *The Looming Student Debt Crisis: Providing Fairness For Struggling Students*, Subcomm. on Administrative Oversight and the Courts of the Senate Judiciary Comm., March 20, 2012. Available at http://www.judiciary.senate.gov/hearings/hearing.cfm?id=eb997a7c3376c76b36a041cf2a10ca10.

[33] *H.R. 5043, the "Private Student Loan Bankruptcy Fairness Act of 2010*, Subcomm. on Commercial and Administrative Law of the H. Comm. on the Judiciary, April 22, 2010. Available at http://judiciary.house.gov/hearings/hear_100422.html.

[34] CRS Report WSLG268, *Revisiting the Treatment of Private Student Loans and Other Educational Benefits in Bankruptcy*, by Carol A. Pettit.

[35] 11 U.S.C. §101 *et seq.*

the term. Currently most courts use the *"Brunner* test."[36] However, application of that test does not appear to be uniform across the courts, particularly when determining whether the first prong of the test is met. Briefly, the *Brunner* test requires each of the following three factors to be satisfied before determining that failure to discharge a student loan in bankruptcy would cause the debtor or the debtor's dependents undue hardship:

1.   inability to maintain a minimum standard of living,

2.   impairment for a significant portion of the repayment period, and

3.   a good faith effort to repay the loans.

Neither the First nor Eighth Circuit Court has adopted the *Brunner* test. The Eighth Circuit has adopted a "totality of the circumstances" test for undue hardship. Although the First Circuit has not explicitly adopted either test, some of its courts have endorsed the totality of the circumstances test.

Noncitizens and Eligibility for HEA Federal Student Aid Programs[37]

The extent to which residents of the United States who are not U.S. citizens should be eligible for federal student aid has been a contentious issue for several decades. This question is especially complex when it comes to educational policies. The U.S. Supreme Court held that a Texas statute that would have prohibited unauthorized student aliens from receiving a free public elementary and secondary education violated the Constitution, but the federal laws restricting noncitizen access to financial aid for higher education have not been successfully challenged. Noncitizen eligibility for HEA aid programs epitomizes this tension.

Background

The United States had 25 million noncitizens in 2010, including 12% who were 18-24 years old and 50% who were 25-44 years old. [38] Noncitizens are much less likely to have graduated from high school or to have no more than a high school education than native born and naturalized U.S. citizens.

Prior to sweeping overhauls of immigration and welfare laws in 1996, lawful permanent residents (LPRs) and other noncitizens who were legally permitted to reside in the United States according to the Immigration and Nationality Act (INA) were generally eligible for federal benefits on the same basis as citizens in programs where rules were established by law or regulation. Unauthorized (illegally present) aliens were barred from participation in all the major federal assistance programs that had statutory provisions for noncitizens, as were aliens legally present in a temporary status (i.e., nonimmigrants, such as persons admitted for tourism, education, or

---

[36] Brunner v. New York State Higher Education Services Corp., 831 F.2d 395, 396 (2d Cir. 1987) (adopting for the circuit the test enunciated in Brunner v. N.Y. State Higher Educ. Serv. Corp., 46 B.R. 752, 756 (S.D.N.Y. 1985).

[37] This section was prepared by Ruth Ellen Wasem, rwasem@crs.loc.gov, 7-7342.

[38] CRS Report R41592, *The U.S. Foreign-Born Population: Trends and Selected Characteristics*, by William A. Kandel.

---

employment). The Higher Education Amendments of 1986 (P.L. 99-498) codified regulations by limiting the eligibility for many federal student aid programs to U.S. citizens and LPRs.

Title IV of the Personal Responsibility and Work Opportunity Reconciliation Act (PRWORA) of 1996 (P.L. 104-193) established comprehensive restrictions on the eligibility of all noncitizens for means-tested public assistance, with exceptions for LPRs with a substantial U.S. work history or military connection. Section 401 of PRWORA further barred foreign nationals who were unauthorized or temporarily present from any "federal public benefit" except the emergency services and programs expressly listed in Section 401(b) of PRWORA. This overarching bar to unauthorized aliens hinges on how broadly the phrase "federal public benefit" is implemented.

The U.S. Department of Education did not identify any of the HEA programs as means-tested federal benefits under PRWORA, essentially retaining policies of the Higher Education Amendments of 1986 that permit all LPRs access to HEA programs. It also kept in place the bar on unauthorized aliens and temporary foreign residents, including international students. Since enactment of the Immigration Reform and Control Act of 1986 (IRCA), the Department of Education has been required to verify the immigration status of applicants for federal financial aid through the Systematic Alien Verification for Entitlements (SAVE) system.

Foreign nationals who are unauthorized minors and young adults brought as children to live in the United States by their parents or other adults pose a particular set of policy challenges. These individuals are sometimes referred to as "unauthorized alien students," or, more colloquially, as "DREAM Act kids" or "DREAMers". According to U.S. Department of Homeland Security (DHS) estimates, there were 1.4 million unauthorized alien children under age 18 living in the United States in January 2011. In addition, there were 1.6 million unauthorized individuals aged 18 to 24, and 3.7 million unauthorized individuals aged 25 to 34. As noted above, these individuals are ineligible for federal student financial aid. A provision enacted in 1996 as part of the Illegal Immigration Reform and Immigrant Responsibility Act (IIRIRA) further discourages states and localities from granting unauthorized aliens certain "postsecondary education benefits."

On June 15, 2012, DHS issued a memorandum announcing that certain individuals who were brought to the United States as children and meet other criteria would be considered for deferred action for two years, subject to renewal. They may be considered "lawfully present" for some very narrow purposes under the INA (such as whether the time in deferred status counts as illegal presence under the grounds of inadmissibility) but are otherwise unlawfully present. Foreign nationals who have been issued temporary employment authorization documents (EADs) may legally obtain social security numbers (SSNs). Possession of a valid EAD or SSN issued for temporary employment, however, does not trigger eligibility for federal programs and services. In other words, foreign nationals who are granted deferred action may be able to work but are not entitled to federally-funded public assistance, except for specified emergency services.

Noncitizen Student Aid Policy Options

Leaders in both chambers of Congress have listed immigration reform as a legislative priority in the 113th Congress. Most policymakers agree that the main issues in "comprehensive immigration reform" (CIR) include among its main components revisions of legal immigration and options to address the millions of unauthorized aliens residing in the country. If the CIR includes provisions to expand legal immigrants' admissions, the issue of whether HEA student aid programs should be considered a means-tested federal benefit under PRWORA may arise.

Proponents of permitting DREAM Act or CIR beneficiaries—if Congress enacts such legislation—to be eligible for some, or perhaps all, HEA aid programs maintain that such a policy would be in the national interest. Public investment in higher education for a sub-population to whom Congress might provide provisional legal residence or LPR status would potentially increase their human capital, which in turn, would be a gain for the U.S. economy, according to this perspective.

Opponents of permitting DREAM Act or CIR beneficiaries—if Congress enacts such legislation—to be eligible for some, or perhaps all, HEA aid programs maintain that such a policy would reward illegal behavior, and become a magnet for future flows of unauthorized aliens. Regarding the potential increase in LPR admission, they point to the public charge ground of inadmissibility under INA §212(a) that excludes aliens who appear "likely at any time to become a public charge." Foreign nationals who would demonstrate financial need and thus be eligible for need-based HEA programs should not be given LPR status, according to this perspective, especially given the current budget constraints.

An alternative option would enable DREAM Act or CIR beneficiaries to be eligible for student loans, federal work-study programs, and services, but would bar them from "gift aid" such as federal Pell Grants and federal supplemental educational opportunity grants. DREAM Act legislation has included such provisions. Advocates of this option maintain that it strikes a balance that fosters higher education without a substantial federal investment.

The CIR legislation that Congress may consider may also require unauthorized aliens who become eligible to legalize their immigration status to pass English language and civics tests, raising the issues of the relationship between immigrant integration and naturalization and federal support for civics instruction and English language acquisition. The policy options of expanding, conditioning, or barring eligibility for federally assisted programs to foreign nationals who might obtain provisional legal residence or LPR status may be weighed as part of CIR and may also arise during HEA or Workforce Investment Act (WIA) [39] reauthorization. These issues are especially germane in the context of scoring (i.e., Congressional Budget Office projections of the costs and savings to the federal budget) the legislation.

Postsecondary Education Tax Policy[40]

The 113th Congress may examine postsecondary education tax benefits as a form of student assistance, looking at the interrelationship between tax benefits and traditional student aid, their budgetary cost, who they benefit, and whether there are duplicative or redundant benefits.

Background

Tax benefits for postsecondary education were first introduced nearly 60 years ago. Most of these benefits were originally structured as deductions and exclusions, which reduce taxable income.

---

[39] Adult education programs, such as English Literacy-Civics Grants, are typically considered secondary education programs. Federal adult education programs are authorized under WIA, Title II. For additional information, see CRS Report R43036, *Adult Education and Family Literacy Act (AEFLA): A Primer*, by Benjamin Collins.

[40] This section was prepared by Margot L. Crandall-Hollick, mcrandallhollick@crs.loc.gov, 7-7582.

Since 1997, education tax benefits have become an increasingly important component of federal postsecondary education policy, and now include tax credits, which directly reduce tax liability.

Fourteen tax benefits are currently available for college students and their parents to help pay for postsecondary education.[41] These tax benefits are a mixture of credits, deductions, exclusions, and other incentives. While these terms are sometimes used interchangeably, they are different. Distinctions between the types of incentives are outlined below.

- **Tax credits** reduce the amount an individual owes in taxes directly, on a dollar for dollar basis. Nonrefundable credits cannot exceed taxes owed, and therefore can only reduce an individual's tax liability to zero. Refundable credits can exceed taxes owed; meaning a taxpayer with no tax liability (including low-income taxpayers) receives the credit amount as a refund check.

- **Tax deductions** reduce the amount of a taxpayer's income that is subject to taxation ("taxable income") by the amount of the deduction. As a result, deductions reduce a taxpayer's tax liability, but only by a percentage of the amount deducted depending on the taxpayer's top or marginal tax bracket.[42]

- **Tax exclusions** are amounts of income that are not included as income for tax purposes because the tax code explicitly excludes—or exempts—them from taxation. Like deductions, their value depends on the taxpayer's tax bracket, meaning higher income taxpayers (who are in higher brackets), receive a larger tax reduction.

Higher education tax benefits can be placed into one of three general categories: incentives for current year expenses, preferential tax treatment of student loans, and incentives for saving for college. The Joint Committee on Taxation (JCT) estimates the cost to the federal government of education tax benefits—the revenue foregone from offering these benefits—to be $187.8 billion between 2013 and 2017.[43]

Discussion of Policy Questions

The 113th Congress may explore options for modifying postsecondary education tax provisions, especially in the context of tax reform. Some of the factors that might be taken into account when considering alternative policy options are discussed below.

Effectiveness of Tax Benefits at Achieving Policy Goals

What is the goal of a particular education tax incentive and how effective is the benefit at achieving that goal? For example, one of the primary goals of education tax incentives is to increase college attendance. Some recent research has indicated that tax-based aid does have an impact on college attendance, but also that a significant proportion of recipients—93%—would

---

[41] For more information, see CRS Report R41967, *Higher Education Tax Benefits: Brief Overview and Budgetary Effects*, by Margot L. Crandall-Hollick.

[42] For example, a $4,000 deduction for someone whose marginal tax bracket is the 10% bracket will result in a $400 reduction in that taxpayer's tax bill. If the taxpayer's marginal tax bracket is the 35% bracket, that $4,000 deduction will result in a $1,400 reduction of their tax bill.

[43] Joint Committee on Taxation, Estimates of Federal Tax For Fiscal Years 2012-2017, February 1, 2013, JCS-1-13.

have attended college in the absence of these benefits.[44] What are the policy goals that education tax benefits are intended to achieve, and how do issues of payment timing, the income level of beneficiaries, and complexity impact the effectiveness of the tax benefits? How does the effectiveness compare to traditional student aid?

Complexity and Duplicative Benefits

Do certain tax benefits have similar purposes with others and if so, is it desirable to consolidate them into fewer more easily administrable benefits? For example, there are currently two incentives designed to encourage saving for higher education. Does the benefit of more savings options outweigh the complexity and confusion that may occur as a result of having similar programs?

Who benefits from these tax incentives?

Tax benefits that are structured as deductions and exclusions tend to provide greater benefit to middle- and upper-income taxpayers, while the partially refundable credits tend to benefit certain low-income taxpayers. In light of concern about the federal budget deficit, do policymakers want to target benefits to particular types of students and if so, do these tax incentives benefit the intended populations?

Interaction with Traditional Student Aid

To what extent should postsecondary education tax benefits be coordinated with traditional federal student aid programs or be designed to target certain types of individuals? Should individuals be permitted to apply benefits received through traditional federal student aid programs and postsecondary education tax benefit programs toward the same postsecondary education expenses? Can the administration of student aid be simplified by providing certain forms of assistance through the tax code?

Tax Treatment of Student Loans

Should changes be made to the tax treatment of interest on student loans? Currently, a tax deduction is available to some individuals for interest paid on federal student loans. Also, for some borrowers, forgiven or discharged federal student loan debt is excluded from income, and hence not taxable. But for other individuals, their discharged student loan debt is considered taxable income. Should these distinctions be maintained? Finally, should there be expanded coordination between the Internal Revenue Service (IRS) and the Department of Education (ED) regarding the repayment of student loans based on borrower income?

---

[44] A 2011 study by Nicholas Turner found that tax based aid (the Hope Tax Credit, the Lifetime Learning Credit, and the Tuition and Fees Above-the-Line Deduction) "increases full-time enrollment in the first two years of college by about 2.2 percentage points (6.7 percent)." According to the study, "If all youths eligible for tax-based aid avail themselves of the programs, then a 7 percent enrollment increase implies that 93 percent of tax-based aid recipients would have enrolled without the tax-based aid subsidy." See Nicholas Turner, "The Effect of Tax-Based Federal Student Aid on College Enrollment," *National Tax Journal*, vol. 64, no. 3 (September 2011), pp. 839-862.

Institutional Quality[45]

The 113th Congress may explore various issues regarding the quality of educational programs and offerings at IHEs, and especially how measures of educational quality factor into determinations of IHEs' eligibility to participate in HEA Title IV federal student aid programs (e.g., Pell grants, student loans).

Background

The HEA, as amended, does not set specific educational quality standards for IHEs; however, it does contain requirements that may indirectly reflect an institution's ability to offer a quality education to students.[46] Given the increasing cost of postsecondary education and students' expanded use of Title IV federal student aid to finance their education, there has been a recent focus on whether students are, in fact, receiving a quality education from the IHEs they attend and whether the federal investment made in postsecondary education (primarily through Title IV aid) is a prudent one.

To participate in Title IV federal student aid programs, individual IHEs must meet several standards that may indirectly reflect educational quality. These standards include requirements related to institutional accreditation, the length of academic programs (e.g., credit hours), and the percentage of revenue a school may derive from Title IV versus non-Title IV funds (i.e., the 90/10 rule). Some or all of these topics may be considered by the 113th Congress.

Accreditation

Under the HEA, IHEs must be accredited by an agency recognized by ED to be eligible to participate in Title IV aid programs.[47] Schools not accredited by such ED-recognized agencies are unable to access billions of dollars in federal funds. Institutional accreditation by an ED-recognized accrediting agency may be considered a measure of institutional quality, because it indicates that an IHE meets at least minimal performance standards and maintains financial stability, as determined by an accrediting agency's review.

Perennially, issues regarding whether accreditation is a true measure of institutional quality arise. A specific issue related to this that Congress may wish to consider concerns whether to refocus the accreditation process on student achievement or student outcome measures, rather than on IHE administrative process reviews. Additionally, should Congress decide to help refocus accreditation on student outcome measures, which student outcome measures might be used (e.g., graduation or job placement rates)?

With the increase in online education, Congress may also address whether accrediting agencies should be required to establish separate standards for distance education. In general, three major issues related to accreditation of distance education have been identified:

---

[45] This section was prepared by Alexandra Hegji, adhegji@crs.loc.gov, 7-8384.

[46] These provisions are often referred to as institutional eligibility requirements. For additional information on institutional eligibility, see CRS Report R43159, *Institutional Eligibility for Participation in Title IV Student Financial Aid Programs*, by Alexandra Hegji and Shannon M. Mahan.

[47] 20 U.S.C. §1001(a)(5).

1. IHEs' ability to identify and prevent student identity fraud;[48]

2. inconsistency in accreditation standards applicable to distance education programs; and

3. a lack of sufficient resources for accrediting agencies to conduct reviews of distance education programs.[49]

In addition to agencies that accredit entire institutions, there are many programmatic accrediting agencies that accredit individual programs within IHEs (e.g., law, nursing). While programmatic accreditation is not a requirement for Title IV eligibility, IHEs may wish to have a program accredited, as many employers require prospective employees to have graduated from an accredited program, and licensure requirements for some occupations in certain states require graduation from an accredited program. Because access to some employers hinges on programmatic accreditation, Congress might explore the development of policies that address the availability of federal student aid to students enrolled in professional programs that lack programmatic accreditation.

Credit Hour

Undergraduate educational programs at public and private nonprofit institutions and at proprietary institutions must meet a minimum amount of instructional time to be eligible to participate in Title IV federal student aid (FSA) programs. Generally, programs are measured in credit hours, which are defined in ED regulations and not in HEA statutory language. A credit hour is typically based on two hours of homework for each hour of class attendance required of a student per week.[50] Historically, the amount of time a student spent on instruction was equated with the quality of education provided (i.e., the more instruction time required, the more a student was expected to learn);[51] however, ED has explicitly stated that there is no implicit "seat time" requirement under the credit hour regulations and that it is used only for federal program purposes, thus, allowing institutions to set their own academic standards.[52]

Given the increase in online course offerings from all types of IHEs and that time spent on coursework completed at a distance cannot necessarily be directly measured by an IHE, Congress may wish to explore the application of instructional time requirements to online course offerings. For example, should instructional time continue to be used as a criterion for Title IV eligibility or should Title IV eligibility be based on other criteria, such as a measure of student outcomes (e.g., persistence and completion rates, job placement rates, cohort default rates)? Also, should the credit hour continue to be defined through ED regulations or should the HEA be amended to include a statutory definition of the credit hour?

---

[48] See U.S. Department of Education, Office of Postsecondary Education, Dear Colleague Letter GEN-11-17, "Fraud in Postsecondary Distance Education Programs - URGENT CALL TO ACTION" October 20, 2011.

[49] See U.S. Government Accountability Office, *Use of New Data Could Help Improve Oversight of Distance Education*, 12-39, November 2011, http://www.gao.gov/assets/590/586340.pdf.

[50] 34 C.F.R. §600.2.

[51] U.S. Department of Education, Office of Postsecondary Education, *Student Financial Assistance and Nontraditional Educational Programs (Including the "12-Hour Rule"): A Report to Congress*, July 2001, p.8.

[52] U.S. Department of Education, Office of Postsecondary Education, "Higher Education, Program Integrity Questions and Answers—Credit Hour," CH-A4.

90/10 Rule

To be Title IV eligible, proprietary institutions must derive at least 10% of the revenue they receive from instructional charges from sources other than Title IV FSA funds.[53] This is known as the 90/10 rule. Sources of non-Title IV revenue include funds paid by a student or on behalf of a student by a 3rd party other than the institution (e.g., earnings, savings, private education loans, and some military and veterans' benefits, such as the Post-9/11 GI Bill program). This rule is used as another indicator of institutional quality, as it has been argued that if proprietary institutions are providing a quality education, then they should be able to attract a certain amount of non-Title IV funds (e.g., students who pay out-of-pocket).[54]

In the 113th Congress, Congress may address issues related to the 90/10 rule, as the 112th Congress saw attempts to amend the provision. Possible issues that could be explored include (1) whether to eliminate, maintain, or modify the percentage of funds proprietary IHEs are allowed to derive from Title IV funds; and (2) whether to continue treating military and veterans' education benefits as non-Title IV revenue.

Additional Issues

On June 30, 2012, the U.S. District Court for the District of Columbia vacated most of the gainful employment rules,[55] and rules related to states' authorization of schools operating within their borders[56] are currently being reviewed by courts. In addition, ED has initiated a new round of negotiated rulemaking to develop new regulations that would define what it means for a program to prepare students for gainful employment in a recognized occupation.[57] When final decisions have been made on these rules, there may be additional issues for Congress to consider.

Postsecondary Education Completion[58]

It is often argued that insufficient numbers or an insufficient proportion of the U.S. population are completing college and obtaining a postsecondary certificate or degree. Moreover, concerns are sometimes raised specifically about low completion rates for individuals from certain racial and ethnic groups, males, and students with disabilities. Common arguments for boosting postsecondary completion are maintaining or improving the collective standard of living given global competition, supporting the vitality of the domestic labor market, promoting economic

---

[53] 20 U.S.C. §1094(a)(24).

[54] Proprietary IHEs were singled out by this rule because when the rule was enacted there was evidence of extensive fraud and abuse at proprietary institutions. Many of these institutions were deemed to be focused on obtaining FSA funds, rather than providing a quality education, and because of this, many students left these institutions without enhanced marketable skills and faced poor employment prospects. CRS Report RL32182, *Institutional Eligibility and the Higher Education Act: Legislative History of the 90/10 Rule and Its Current Status*, by Rebecca R. Skinner.

[55] For detailed information about the gainful employment regulations, see CRS Report R42011, *Department of Education Final Rules for Postsecondary Education Programs That Prepare Students for Gainful Employment in a Recognized Occupation*, by David P. Smole.

[56] 20 U.S.C. §1001.

[57] U.S. Department of Education, Office of Postsecondary Education, "Negotiated Rulemaking Committee, Negotiator Nominations and Schedule of Committee Meetings-Title IV Federal Student Aid Programs, Gainful Employment in a Recognized Occupation", 78 *Federal Register* 73, June 12, 2013, pp. 35179-35181.

[58] This section was prepared by Cassandria Dortch, cdortch@crs.loc.gov, 7-0376.

---

well-being of individuals, enhancing democracy, and achieving a return on the federal investment in postsecondary education programs.

As the mean educational attainment in foreign countries continues to rise, there is concern that the competitiveness of the U.S. workforce for jobs that rely on a more educated workforce will decline and lead to a potential lowering of the current and comparative standard of living in the United States. Notwithstanding foreign competition, domestic employers have been increasing their expectations of workers' skill levels and postsecondary credentials. Increasing levels of education are also associated with increased civic participation, which furthers the U.S. democratic tradition.

While over the past half century the federal government has made available billions of dollars in support of improving access to postsecondary education through college preparation programs and federal student aid, authorized by the Higher Education Act and other laws, the policy conversation is shifting toward increasing postsecondary completion. Several potential policy approaches that might be considered as means of supporting further increases in college completion are identified below. These are grouped into the following broad investment categories: postsecondary education preparation, postsecondary institutions, and postsecondary students.

Policy Options

Invest in Pre-college Programs

- Support efforts designed to support preparation for postsecondary education within secondary schools.

- Support programs that aim to ease the transition from secondary to postsecondary institutions through methods such as co-locating institutions or automatically transitioning secondary completers to postsecondary institutions as from elementary to secondary school.

- Support efforts to encourage and prepare adults to return to or enter and succeed in postsecondary education.

- Improve public understanding of college costs and financing.

Invest in Postsecondary Institutions

- Support or require efforts that aim to ensure postsecondary educational institutions have the capacity to graduate a higher proportion of their entrants.

- Provide incentives or rewards to programs and institutions that decrease time to completion, particularly among various population groups (i.e., males, underrepresented groups, English learners, individuals with disabilities).

- Support efforts by postsecondary faculty that improve student retention and completion.

- Hold institutions accountable for student completion-related outcomes.

- Support or require research, evaluation, dissemination, and implementation of methods to measure and increase college completions, from postsecondary credential to degree.

Invest in Postsecondary Students

- Encourage granting maximum college credit and transfer credit for experience, prior coursework, and assessment.

- Support student support services such as transportation, child care, tutoring, mentoring, advising, and counseling to reduce the obstacles to college completion.

- Provide incentives or rewards such as performance-based scholarships to individuals who persist and complete college.

- Encourage the development and implementation of strategies and programs that accommodate a broader range of student learning styles, academic preparation, demographics, and attendance patterns.

Campus Safety[59] [60]

Safeguarding the security of students while they pursue a postsecondary education is a paramount concern of federal, state, and local governments, as well as the institutions that enroll these students. Shootings at institutions of higher education, and by individuals enrolled in IHEs, have heightened congressional concern about school and IHE security. These tragedies have prompted a serious examination by the Obama Administration and ED as to whether everything that can be done to secure schools and IHEs is being done.

Clery Act

While the HEA does not authorize specific programs to address campus crime and security issues, Section 485(f) of Title IV of the HEA contains statutory requirements related to campus crime and security, known collectively as the Jeanne Clery Disclosure of Campus Security Policy and Campus Crime Statistics Act (the Clery Act).

Institutions must comply with Clery Act requirements in order to participate in the federal student aid programs and other programs authorized by Title IV (e.g., Pell Grants). As part of these requirements, each institution is required to submit an annual security report to ED that provides information about campus security policies and campus crime statistics. IHEs are also required to make this information available to all current students and employees and to any prospective students or employees, upon request. IHEs do not receive specific funding from the federal

---

[59] This section was prepared by Jody Feder, jfeder@crs.loc.gov, 7-8088; and Gail McCallion, gmccallion@crs.loc.gov, 7-7758.

[60] For more detailed information on school and campus security see CRS Report RL33980, *School and Campus Safety Programs and Requirements in the Elementary and Secondary Education Act and Higher Education Act*, by Gail McCallion and Rebecca R. Skinner.

government to aid in compliance with these requirements. However, ED has published a resource for IHEs on the requirements of the Clery Act.[61]

Privacy Issues

Some observers are concerned that the Family Educational Rights and Privacy Act (FERPA) could pose a barrier to efforts to improve campus safety. Under FERPA, IHEs that receive federal funds are prohibited from releasing student education records without prior written consent.[62] Because educational records encompass student health records, including mental health records, there have been concerns that FERPA may prevent school officials from disclosing information about students who may pose a threat to others. Although FERPA does contain an exception that allows education records to be released in connection with an emergency if the records are necessary to protect the health or safety of the student or others,[63] some commentators have questioned whether this exception is too narrow. Indeed, after the shootings at Virginia Tech, Congress attempted to clarify FERPA's health or safety exception by amending the HEA to require ED to provide guidance clarifying rules regarding disclosure when a "student poses a significant risk of harm to himself or herself or to others, including a significant risk of suicide, homicide, or assault." Such guidance must clarify that institutions that disclose such information in good faith are not liable for the disclosure.[64]

Civil Rights Issues

Bullying and harassment have also been linked to school and IHE safety.[65] Although student bullying may be barred by state or local laws or by individual schools, current federal law does not explicitly prohibit such bullying.[66] Under certain circumstances, however, federal civil rights statutes may be used to combat bullying in schools. For example, several statutes make it unlawful for educational programs or activities that receive federal funds, such as those operated by IHEs that participate in the Title IV student financial aid programs, to discriminate on the basis of race, color, national origin, disability, or sex.[67] One type of discrimination prohibited under

---

[61] This resource is titled the "Handbook for Campus Crime Reporting." It provides procedures, examples, and references for IHEs to use in complying with the Clery Act requirements. See http://www2.ed.gov/admins/lead/safety/handbook.pdf.

[62] 20 U.S.C. §1232g.

[63] 20 U.S.C. §1232g(b)(1)(I).

[64] P.L. 110-315, §801. The Department of Education subsequently issued regulations to similar effect. Department of Education, Family Educational Rights and Privacy, 73 FR 74806 (December 9, 2008).

[65] Some research indicates that both victims of bullying and those who engage in bullying behavior can experience both short and long-term effects resulting in psychological difficulties and social relationship problems. A GAO literature review of seven meta-analyses on the impact of bullying on victims found that bullying could result in psychological, physical, academic, and behavioral issues. Government Accountability Office, *School Bullying: Extent of Legal Protections for Vulnerable Groups Needs to Be More Fully Assessed*, GA0-12-349, May 2012, pp. 8-10, http://www.gao.gov/assets/600/591202.pdf. In addition, a Secret Service study on school safety and school attacks found that "Many attackers felt bullied, persecuted or injured by others prior to the attack." Vossekuil, B., et al., The Final Report and Findings of the Safe School Initiative: Implications for the Prevention of School Attacks in the United States, Department of Education and Secret Service, Washington D.C. 2004, p. 12.

[66] If a bully assaults another student or engages in other criminal action, then there may be criminal or tort laws that apply.

[67] See, for example, Title VI of the Civil Rights Act of 1964, 42 U.S.C. §§2000d et seq; Section 504 of the Rehabilitation Act of 1973, 29 U.S.C. §794; and Title IX of the Education Amendments of 1972, 20 U.S.C. §§1681 et (continued...)

---

these laws is peer harassment—also known as bullying—but only if such harassment is sufficiently serious that it creates a so-called hostile environment and only if the bullying is encouraged, tolerated, or ignored by school officials. That means that if bullying both rises to this level and involves discrimination or harassment on the basis of race, color, national origin, sex, or disability, then it would be prohibited by federal law. Other types of bullying would not be covered.

In 2010, ED issued guidance that discusses when student bullying or harassment may violate federal education anti-discrimination laws and that clarifies a school's obligation to combat such bullying or harassment.[68] The guidance includes a discussion of when bullying or harassment that targets lesbian, gay, bisexual, or transgender students may be a form of sex discrimination that violates Title IX, as well as a section that describes when bullying or harassment of students who share a particular religion may constitute national origin discrimination in violation of Title VI.

Policy Options

In response to concerns about campus safety, the 113th Congress may wish to consider a variety of legislative options to address the issue, including, but not limited to the following:

- Providing federal funding to assist IHEs in developing and implementing emergency management plans.

- Increasing access to mental health services for students.

- Providing federal funding for initiatives to reduce bullying and harassment at IHEs.

- Enacting federal legislation to explicitly prohibit bullying on college campuses.

- Providing federal funding to IHEs to increase campus security.

- Amending FERPA to clarify or expand the circumstances under which a student's mental health records may be disclosed without consent.

- Prohibiting discrimination on the basis of sexual orientation, gender identity, and religion in educational programs or activities.

(...continued)

seq.

[68] United States Department of Education, *Office for Civil Rights*, Dear Colleague Letter, October 26, 2010, http://www2.ed.gov/about/offices/list/ocr/letters/colleague-201010 html.

Author Contact Information

David P. Smole, Coordinator
Specialist in Education Policy
dsmole@crs.loc.gov, 7-0624

Adam Stoll
Section Research Manager
astoll@crs.loc.gov, 7-4375

Shannon M. Mahan
Specialist in Education Policy
smahan@crs.loc.gov, 7-7759

Carol A. Pettit
Legislative Attorney
cpettit@crs.loc.gov, 7-9496

Ruth Ellen Wasem
Specialist in Immigration Policy
rwasem@crs.loc.gov, 7-7342

Cassandria Dortch
Analyst in Education Policy
cdortch@crs.loc.gov, 7-0376

Margot L. Crandall-Hollick
Analyst in Public Finance
mcrandallhollick@crs.loc.gov, 7-7582

Alexandra Hegji
Analyst in Social Policy
adhegji@crs.loc.gov , 7-8384

Jody Feder
Legislative Attorney
jfeder@crs.loc.gov, 7-8088

Gail McCallion
Specialist in Social Policy
gmccallion@crs.loc.gov, 7-7758